PROPERTY OF

_____

POLLINATOR ✻ COLLECTION

INSIGHTS
an imprint of
INSIGHT ◉ EDITIONS
www.insighteditions.com

Copyright © 2022 Insight Editions.
All rights reserved.

MANUFACTURED IN CHINA
10 9 8 7 6 5 4 3 2

PROPERTY OF

POLLINATOR ✹ COLLECTION

INSIGHTS
an imprint of
INSIGHT 👁 EDITIONS
www.insighteditions.com

Copyright © 2022 Insight Editions.
All rights reserved.

MANUFACTURED IN CHINA

10 9 8 7 6 5 4 3 2

PROPERTY OF

_____

POLLINATOR ✸ COLLECTION

INSIGHTS
an imprint of
INSIGHT 👁 EDITIONS
www.insighteditions.com

Copyright © 2022 Insight Editions.
All rights reserved.

MANUFACTURED IN CHINA

10 9 8 7 6 5 4 3 2